SURVIVORS
—————— of a ——————
GENERATION UNHEARD

Stories of Generational Survivors

Compiled by Saadia White

Published in Hampton, VA, by Fruition Publishing Concierge Services. Fruition Publishing Concierge Services is a division of Alesha Brown, LLC. www.FruitionPublishing.com

Fruition Publishing Concierge Services can bring authors to your live event. For more information or to book an event, visit Fruition Publishing Concierge Services at www.FruitionPublishing.com.

ISBN 978-1-7338917-1-4 paperback

Library of Congress Control Number: 2019909429

DEDICATION

This book is dedicated to my mother, Renee Steedley. Proceeds of this book will go to the **Renee Steedley Family Residence shelter**.

Who was RENEE STEEDLEY?
(Shared from http://www.aapci.org/services/renne.html#)

Every now and then, we meet people in life whom we develop an immediate attachment to. Renee Steedley was such an individual. A contract manager with the NYC Department of Homeless Services, she was also a wife, a mother, a daughter and a dear friend. Renee was an advocate for the homeless and a supporter of all AAPCI's (African American Planning Commission Inc.) endeavors. She was always bright eyed and bushy tailed-a beautiful smile and a warm hug for anyone who needed it.

We all miss you Renee. Rest in Peace.

-AAPCI

Renee Steedley Family Residence is a temporary haven for survivors of domestic violence. Opened on June 30, 2017 and funded by the New York City Human Resources Administration ("HRA"), the Renee Steedley Family Residence is a transitional Tier II domestic violence residence.

The mission of the Renee Steedley Family Residence is to offer survivors and their minor children, a safe but temporary haven in which to pick up the pieces of their shattered lives.

The secondary goal of the Renee Steedley Family Residence is to prepare families for independent living, assist them in locating permanent housing within or outside the State of New York, and to offer a host of on- and off-site supportive services that will help empower victims and minimize the root causes of domestic violence.

The Renee Steedley Family Residences offers survivors (regardless of gender, race, culture, religion, ethnic background or sexual preference) the opportunity to reside in a secured environment for up to six months or more as needed. The program is culturally sensitive to allow families to feel immediately at home and to foster ethnic pride in children and family members.

The Renee Steedley Family Residence is able to accommodate families including those with adolescent children, up to 18 years of age, and male head-of-household. The Renee Steedley Family Residence provides temporary accommodations with on-site social services to 54 homeless parents. During their stay, each family is housed in a furnished studio, one or two bedroom, fully furnished apartment, depending upon family configuration. All applicants are domestic violence survivors with children and reside outside of the Renee Steedley Family Residence catchment area. All families have access to onsite social services that address the psychological and concrete causes and effects of domestic violence, homelessness and unemployment.

PROLOGUE

I know there are many stories written about abuse survivors and their horrific encounters. While this book includes those, even the graphic and disgusting details, it also includes something that many of them do not:

> **Expert clinical analysis of, and interview with, each survivor**

Dr. Sarah Williams, Licensed and Board Certified Clinical Psychotherapist, serves as the Clinical Trauma Specialist for *Survivors of a Generation Unheard: Stories of Generational Survivors.* Dr. Sarah Williams is the owner of Covenant Way Clinical Counseling where she helps individuals cope with mental health as well as lift the stigma of mental illness bringing others from darkness to light. (Learn more about her and the celebrity work she does at the end of this book.)

Let's face it: as hard as it is to talk about the trauma you survived, it is even harder to recognize the help you need. Seeking professional help, especially counseling, comes with a stigma that many survivors would rather avoid. The problem with this approach is that it keeps one imprisoned in a never-ending emotional, mental and invisible prison that is 100% avoidable.

Whether you are a generational survivor or know one, you are invited to take this journey of transparency and healing. We must save the next generations from the ravages of abuse by any means necessary. Silence is deadly.

Compiled by
SAADIA WHITE

SURVIVORS
OF A
GENERATION
UNHEARD

Stories of Generational Survivors

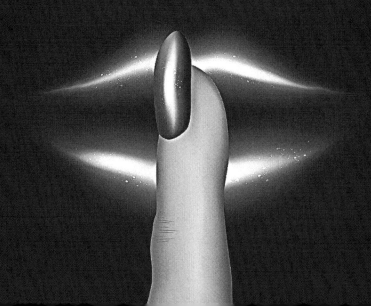

Table of Contents

* * *

Compiled by
SAADIA WHITE

SURVIVORS
— OF A —
GENERATION
UNHEARD

Stories of Generational Survivors

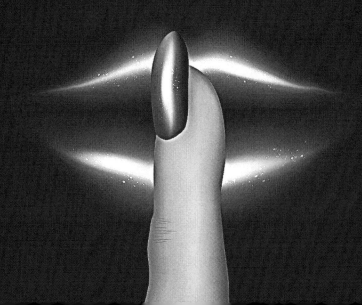

Introduction

———⊂∞•∞⊃———

"**N**oooo! Please don't hurt her; please stop!" The muffled sounds of a young girl's cries from a distance. But you can't hear her voice because her cries are drowned out by the wailing screams of the beaten woman bouncing off the wall next to her. The sounds on the little girl's wall are thunderous, but in an instant, all is DEATHLY quiet.

This was not the first time that little girl has heard those shrill screams or pounding sounds. Those sounds would become repetitive beats in her head like a drummer beating his drum. The wailing screamer would eventually crack open the little girl's door and peek in with her pale, light face covered with black and blue bruises and broken blue and red eye vessels. The woman peeking into the room was my mother and the little girl… you guessed it, was me!

I AM SAADIA WHITE–A GENERATIONAL SURVIVOR!

There has been a lot of confusion surrounding the meaning behind who or what a *generational survivor* is. The term *generational survivor* is not to be confused with *generational curses, although* what a generational survivor has been through could be due to a generational curse. *A generational survivor is an individual who has witnessed–or has been a part of during their childhood–domestic, emotional, physical, verbal and*

1

sexual abuse, whether it stemmed from the biological parents, guardians or immediate family members. There have been many generations of children who have witnessed the brutal beatings of a family member and I was one of them.

At the age of seven, I witnessed my mother being choked. With one hand, *The Monster in our house* lifted her by her neck, feet off the ground and dangling in the air. I cannot tell you the reason why he did this, but then again, why should there be a reason for this "act of insanity"?

What does a child say or do when he/she see his/her loved one hurt, wounded and in need of help? I felt hopeless as a child, watching my mother—the women who brought me into this world; my nurturer and protector—suffer at the hands of a man who had no soul. He surely was heartless. I viewed him as the *Ice King when* I was young. Today I realize that my perception of him gave him way too much POWER over my mind, body and soul.

The barbaric beatings my mother suffered at the hands of *The Monster went on for what seemed like a lifetime. I never felt safe, happy or comfortable in my own home. Any time my mother would leave me with The Monster, I tried to not make a sound. I would tiptoe around my room, playing with my baby doll, scared to breathe even the slightest breath. But on one Saturday morning when my mother left for work, The Monster called me into my mother's room. I figured that he knew how badly I wanted to watch cartoons. This would be the first time, but not the last that he violated me.*

At the hands of one of my mother's boyfriends, *The Monster, I was molested.* He stole my innocence that day; my purity was stolen and tainted by the hands of a *monster*. After it was over, I knew that I was different and I didn't know quite how to feel. *The Monster made me play with him as he played with me—making me perform oral sex on him even after I urinated on* myself.

He continued to enjoy the pleasure he derived from taking advantage of my innocence and he used the typical statement that all predators use: "Say anything to anyone and I will kill you and your mother." I developed an emptiness that seemed to follow me through my teen and adult years. My self-esteem was significantly low and I definitely did not value myself at all.

The sexual trauma I experienced as a child was the gateway to my sexual deviant behavior. I didn't know how to be romantic and never stayed in a relationship for longer than a couple of months. What was love really? My relationships in my young adulthood could be referred to as *sexcapades.*

I became a teen mom to a baby boy when I was 16 years old. My son's father, who was slightly older than me, would be the one who actually penetrated me and took my virginity. I considered myself already "housebroken" by that time and knew more about oral sex than any 16-year-old should. That was just the beginning.

My version of love was perverted and something from a horror scene. What I saw as a child never left me and, in some ways, a portion of me was stuck as that frightened seven-year-old girl. As a teenager, I was troubled and so misunderstood and no one knew why (not even my mother). I constantly ran away from home even after my mother moved on from The Monster. My final time running away would be in the 7th grade. I went missing for almost three weeks! When the police finally found me and brought me to the station-house, my mother, stepfather and father were all there waiting for me.

The detectives placed me in a small room with my father, whom I hadn't seen in years, but for some reason, I felt safe for the first time. The detectives asked me why I kept running away. With tears streaming down my face, I told them everything from my mother's brutal beatings to the sexual molestation I endured. By the time I was done, my dad was out of his seat and ready to beat my new stepfather. I had to explain to him and the police officers that it wasn't my current stepfather that molested me but one of my mother's previous boyfriends.

When the detectives told my mom what I shared with them, she called me "a liar seeking attention." Her refusal to believe me deeply hurt me. I can remember being so angry with my mother that I felt a deep hatred toward her. She was my mother who was supposed to protect me but failed to do so. My relationship with my mother was spoiled like a container of curdled milk gone bad.

Life was a blur for me after that: I was wounded and needed to feel something, anything. I tried to kill myself, but I felt the need to protect others from the type of predator that violated me. Several times as a teen and as an adult, I turned to alcohol as a coping mechanism for my pain and depression. I can recall drinking heavily at age 14. Alcohol was my comfort zone; my friend when I was alone in my room and the demons surrounded me. I was not only dependent upon alcohol, but I was also a sex fiend.

Since I was no longer a virgin at age 16, I needed sex to take me to the highest form of power that I longed to possess (or so I thought). I wanted to have control over something in my life and I foolishly thought that indulging in my *sexcapades was the answer. But it never was. I was a lost, wild child with an ignorant plan of revenge, but on who? My abuser? My mother? The manipulative men I had encountered on my journey of* justice?

This is just a small piece of my journey as a *generational survivor. I needed therapy as a form of healing* (which helped), but my *survival wasn't* a factor until I found JESUS CHRIST and decided to become a living vessel and servant for CHRIST. I was his child and I accepted Jesus as my LORD and SAVIOR. On that day, and that day only, I was freed from the chains of bad memories and injustice that held me in bondage.

Healing was truly a struggle and sometimes still is. I am a married woman with children scarred by a disfigurement deep within my soul. My husband and I talk a lot about what I have gone through and that really helps. We discuss my triggers—yes I have triggers or *events or objects that remind me of or subconsciously connect me to an aspect of my abuse. My walk with CHRIST placed me right where I needed to be and prepared me for the journey ahead. I guess* you can say that Christ has been preparing me my whole life.

I know there are many more generational survivors out there, men and women, and I implore you to face yourself and release the mask you hide behind. If you don't, you will destroy the essence who you are that lies beneath all the scar tissue, hurt and pain. Use your pain to prevail and as an instrument of empowerment. Remember and repeat this affirmation: I AM NOT MY PAST.

I AM SAADIA WHITE–A GENERATIONAL SURVIVOR!

TELL YOUR STORY

What part of this story resonates the most with you?

_____

_____

_____

Have you seen signs of this abuse in your family?

_____

_____

_____

In what ways did you respond to the trauma that was thrust upon you
like this survivor?

_____

_____

_____

_____

TELL YOUR STORY (continued)

What cries went unheard (verbal and nonverbal)?

_____

_____

_____

_____

What signs of a predator were ignored?

_____

_____

_____

_____

_____

What were your key takeaways from this survivor's story?

_____

_____

_____

_____

_____

Compiled by
SAADIA WHITE

SURVIVORS
OF A
GENERATION
UNHEARD

Stories of Generational Survivors

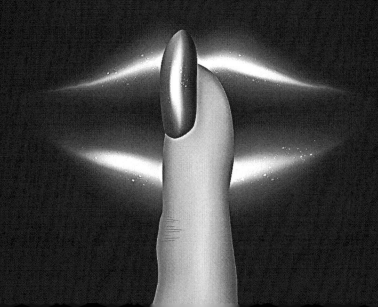

The Psychology Behind *Generational Survivor*

Saadia is a Generational Survivor of Molestation

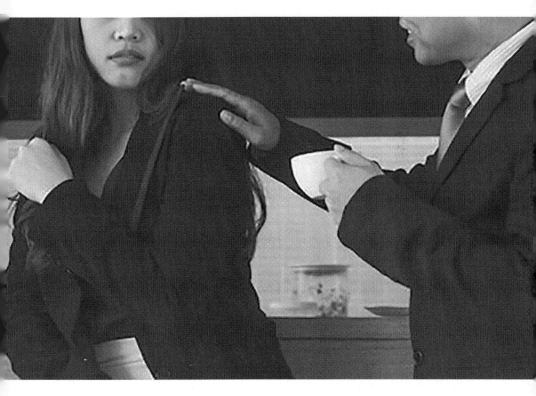

Fear, terror and confusion formulated the baseline of Saadia's childhood. Initially, hearing and witnessing the violent abuse of her mother and later becoming a victim of sexual molestation, all equate to trauma.

The vicarious victimization alone was enough to impact Saadia's emotional well-being and the course of her adult decisions. In addition, Saadia became a victim of horrendous sexual molestation that resulted in her confusion and inability to form healthy relationships with others. As a result, she told herself that she was not worthy of love.

Saadia cried out and desperately needed her Mom to believe her. Because of her Mom's disbelief and lack of support, Saadia believed that no one would ever believe or support her.

Dr. Sarah Williams, NCC, LPC, EAS-C
Licensed and Board Certified Clinical Psychotherapist
Clinical Trauma Specialist for *Survivors of a Generation Unheard*

Break The Stigma

Dr. Sarah's Interview with Saadia White

How has the victimization affected your ability to relate to and/or trust others?

I feel as though I give all of me first. I give me first because I don't want people to experience what I went through. Often times, I don't exercise the wisdom necessary to protect me from further harm. I try to be a hero and not a victim.

Did you experience post-traumatic disorders such as Anxiety, Depression, Personality Disorder, Suicidal, Self- Injury?

I struggled with Anxiety and Depression. The trauma was complicated by my Mother not believing me when I reported the abuse to the police.

At what point, age, stage or moment did you move from Victim to Generational Survivor?

I was a teenage runaway. I ran from my problems often. I came to a point that I couldn't keep running. I needed to be a winner not a runner. Last year I came into myself. When I coined the term Generational Survivor. I realized that I am no longer the "unforeseen" victim. I am a Generational Survivor. I had to re-think the whole process. I have overcome so much and by owning my pain I moved forward. I entered the next level when I developed the term Generational Survivor.

What steps did you take to process your healing?

I had to speak the words out loud. By having the chance to tell my story and telling it, the healing process was able to take place. In addition, deep prayer with God and my relationship with my husband and my children helped me to heal.

What advice can you give to others?

Get a connection and understand your hurt-get to the root of the hurt. You have to open up and share your story. Even taking the chance of not being believed is better than not sharing at all. Have a strong connection with yourself and a strong relationship with God. Get to know yourself and forgive yourself. Most importantly, do away with any thoughts of blame for the victimization.

Clinical Perspective

**Saadia has exemplified Generational Survivorship
from Molestation and Vicarious Trauma.**

Watching her Mother endure physical abuse and later becoming a victim herself, Saadia experienced horrendous helplessness. This experience was further complicated by the experience of not being believed once she reported the molestation. From her trauma, Saadia chose Law Enforcement as a career. She also works tirelessly in her community. The *Survivors of a Generation Unheard could've easily been reserved for herself, however, she enthusiastically desires* to allow the voice of others to be heard. In that sense, because her voice went on death ears, she has a goal of ensuring that others are not just heard, but also acknowledged for the truth in their trauma.

Interview Completed by:

**Dr. Sarah Williams, NCC, LPC, EAS-C
Licensed and Board Certified Clinical Psychotherapist
Clinical Trauma Specialist for *Survivors of a Generation Unheard***

Break The Stigma

Compiled by
SAADIA WHITE

SURVIVORS
OF A
GENERATION
UNHEARD

Stories of Generational Survivors

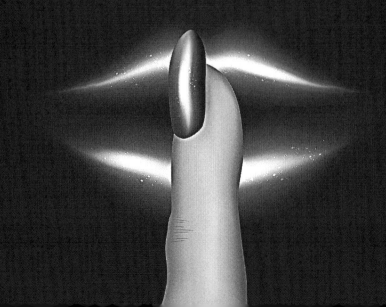

The Hidden Tears
By Sandra Sakponou

Compiled by
SAADIA WHITE

SURVIVORS
— OF A —
GENERATION
UNHEARD

Stories of Generational Survivors

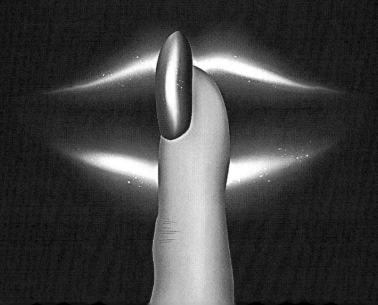

The Hidden Tears by Sandra Sakponou

---◦∞◦---

> *Sometimes in life, circumstances happen that we think would never happen to us. It's important to understand that some people care more about your experiences than they do about your opinion. Anyone can have an opinion, but only experiences lead to change. Experiences lead to change, change proceeds to opportunities, including an opportunity to gain courage.*
>
> *-Sandra Sakponou*

On June 22, 1992, at 3:00 am, I gave birth to a healthy, beautiful baby girl who weighed eight pounds. I looked at her and named her Essenam which means *God heard my prayers*. One of the happiest moments in a woman's life only left me asking, *how will we make it? How will she survive?*

I was so young and naïve to be the mother of an innocent baby girl born into a world full of wickedness. Living a life with no guidance, without a mother or a strong person to guide you, places you in a world filled with hurt. As time went on, I learned that living in this sort of environment, although painful, provided a learning experience that strengthens you, humbles you and builds you to a place that surpasses your struggles. And my struggles at the time of Essenam's birth were great.

I slept on a floor for the nine months I carried her. Now where would she rest her head? I knew the pain and discomfort from sleeping on a floor with no cushion between your body and the hard surface. What clothes would I dress her in? I only had one top and one wrapper that I wore. The baby needed clothes and a bed to sleep in. Would they let me sleep on a bed with her? The answer was no and there was nothing I could say or do about it.

I had three days—three days to learn everything I needed to know about raising a baby. I had to learn how to breastfeed and bathe her while my body was racked with pain and I was hungry. I wished for food to eat since I felt so physically weak. There are no words to describe the amount of abuse the innocent girl within me endured. I remember hearing my baby cry and not being able to touch or hold her until I finished whatever task I was working on. My heart and spirit felt the pain of my innocent child. The pain I felt was indescribable, but no one recognized it because they were so busy abusing me.

I became the maid that would do everything from laundry to housework without complaints. I needed enough food so that I would have milk in my breasts. Some days I felt dizzy and tired; so much so that I couldn't do anything and I was beaten as a result. On those days I was denied food. On one occasion, my nephew bought me food after seeing what I was going through. He even fought with his mom and sister to stop all they had been doing to me because he simply couldn't stand to see me in such a weakened state. My relief came from the father of the guy who raped me.

I was *blessed with $10 by the father of my rapist and my cousin gave me $5. I used the money to start selling meat pies to generate some income to feed my baby and me. Despite my efforts, I never stopped wondering how my baby's and my life would turn out.*

Questions ran through my mind about what the future held in store for me and my baby. I asked myself should I stop being abused and go back to school, which would bring another level of abuse. Was staying and dealing with the abuse a better option? I came to the conclusion that enough was enough and I decided to go back to the village, but I still couldn't answer what I would do or how my baby and I would survive.

One evening I went to the dad that raised me and told him I wanted to return to school. I told him I deserved a better life and I needed to create a better future for my baby. The courage I had to tell him that was unheard of in my village, especially for my age. My dad didn't get it and the only question he asked was, *did you tell your mom? I replied no because I knew she wouldn't support* my decision. She was ready to send me to my rapist's parents (according to our customs, I was automatically considered his wife). I told my mom *over my dead body*.

My dad asked me again, what about the baby? I replied that I had no idea, but I knew I had to go back to school. When he asked me what items I needed, I said only a book and pen. He told me to give him time to think and I immediately contacted the principal of my school. He accepted me, according to him, because of my courage and he didn't request school fees. However, the real battle awaited with my mother.

My mind raced, wondering what I would say to her and how she would respond. The anticipation was too much and I went to her and let it all out. I unleashed a stream of insults, hateful and abusive words, on my mom. I had no fear because I knew my dad wouldn't let me down. I was willing to risk starvation to avoid listening to her, but my dad gave me money to eat when she refused to give me food. Sometimes we had to sell everything we owned, but she would retaliate by locking the door so

I couldn't enter the house. She forgot that a day would come where she would need someone to take care of her, which I have been doing since I left that country.

Months and days passed by and, before I knew it, I was back in school which presented new challenges. My daughter was only four months old at the time and, although I adored my beautiful smiling baby, my aunt who raised me was already against my return. Where would I go from there?

I still remember preparing to return to school and my dad giving me $10 to buy school supplies. He agreed to take care of my baby while I attended school and even one of my nieces helped him (may they both rest in peace). I returned to school seeing the shock on the teachers' faces. Those were challenging times as I was exhausted, balancing a crying baby and homework, especially during the first year. Despite the difficulty, including not having food at times, I became a role model to many. I refused to give up and, once I made it through the first semester, I gained the motivation I needed to keep going.

Sharing this period of my life with you is life changing for me. I never shared my story before and what better time to share it than when I'm ready to take on the world. I want to not only heal my heavy heart, but inspire others to come out of the shadow of fear. Everything happens for a reason, but it's up to us to make that reason powerful, reachable and meaningful.

Yesterday I was a rape victim—a victim of domestic violence and an abuse victim—abused by the people that were supposed to protect me. I was a girl that was removed from her parents at age two and never knew her parents until age 14. I was a stay-at-home mom of five that always believed she was ugly and illiterate and allowed those labels to affect her entire life.

Today I take back all my power and rebuild myself to empower the world. I encourage you to just believe that change is possible, but only if you embrace it with your full heart and are willing to trust the process. Believe in yourself because you are enough when you know your worth.

TELL YOUR STORY

What part of this story resonates the most with you?

_____

_____

_____

Have you seen signs of this abuse in your family?

_____

_____

_____

In what ways did you respond to the trauma that was thrust upon you like this survivor?

_____

_____

_____

_____

TELL YOUR STORY (continued)

What cries went unheard (verbal and nonverbal)?

_____

_____

_____

_____

What signs of a predator were ignored?

_____

_____

_____

_____

What were your key takeaways from this survivor's story?

_____

_____

_____

_____

The Psychology Behind The Hidden Tears
Sandra is a Generational Survivor of Rape and Abuse

For Sandra, she has known abuse for probably as long as she has known her name. Her experience, unfortunately, is a common one for a child that has experienced sexual trauma.

Sandra describes her life as one cemented in loneliness and isolation. Even when in the presence of others, she finds it difficult to feel accepted and a part of a group. She learned at an early age to exist without love and support.

Dr. Sarah Williams, NCC, LPC, EAS-C
Licensed and Board Certified Clinical Psychotherapist
Clinical Trauma Specialist for *Survivors of a Generation Unheard*

Break The Stigma

Dr. Sarah's Interview with Sandra Sakponou

<u>How has the victimization affected your ability to relate to and/or trust others?</u>

I hesitate before I get close. My spirit has to connect with a person before I can trust. I have a fear of getting close to others. To avoid closeness, I make up jokes to cover those feelings of fear of being hurt. I have been hurt a lot. I don't have friends; I don't go out.

<u>Did you experience post-traumatic disorders such as Anxiety, Depression, PD, Suicidal, Self- Injury?</u>

At the time of the rape I was 14. I went through a deep Depression and to comfort myself I made a friend with a tree. I would listen to birds. I would take a book with me and write. I also started playing soccer and running. I used to talk too much in class to cope with my depression and loneliness.

At what point, age, stage, or moment did you move from Victim to Generational Survivor?

There was a time period when I would experience abuse and when my daughter starting cutting herself. I realized I had to stand up for myself. I had to stand up alone and fight this battle.

What steps did you take to process your healing?

I go out some time at 4:00 am and meditate. Physical activity such as the gym, boxing, running, as well as writing poems helped me to process my healing.

What advice can you give others?

It is important to remember that our freedom does not come from people. Your tears are your strength and your power. Stand up against the hurt and down the road you will find healing. Never let anyone break you. You have to know how to let go of the pain. Stay and fight don't run from the problem.

Clinical Perspective

Sandra has exemplified Generational Survivorship from Rape and Abuse. Healing from a traumatic boundary violation such as rape is an ongoing process. With each day, Sandra is learning about herself. By working on her physical health, nutrition and mental wellness, Sandra heals by speaking out and empowering others.

Sandra freely admits that she allows herself to cry healing tears. The release is cleansing of the soul and freeing for Sandra. The young girl that had to make friends with a tree to combat loneliness is now surrounded by dozens of women that have a shared experience. Sandra can now smile and gain the freedom that exists from the release of her tears.

Interview Completed by:

Dr. Sarah Williams, NCC, LPC, EAS-C
Licensed and Board Certified Clinical Psychotherapist
Clinical Trauma Specialist for *Survivors of a Generation Unheard*

Break The Stigma

Compiled by
SAADIA WHITE

SURVIVORS
— OF A —
GENERATION
UNHEARD

Stories of Generational Survivors

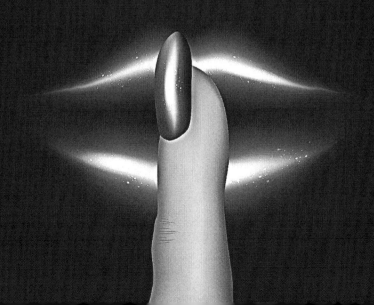

Casualties of War
By Gloria Henderson

Compiled by
SAADIA WHITE

SURVIVORS
— OF A —
GENERATION
UNHEARD

Stories of Generational Survivors

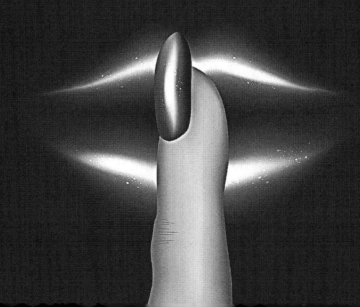

Casualties of War by Gloria Henderson

At seven years old, I witnessed physical abuse for the first time when my mother married my stepfather. My mother, older brother, younger sister and I came to the United States courtesy of him.

Prior to the abuse, life for me as a young child was exciting, especially coming to this country. I was a happy, spirited and bright child. I loved seeing animated characters on TV for the first time; loved learning the English language and loved laughing and playing jokes. I was as happy as any child could be until my stepfather returned from Vietnam. I now believe that my stepfather's Vietnam experiences unleashed pure hell into our home.

I witnessed my mother being pushed through a glass door by my stepfather. I do not recall the severity of mother's injuries, although the nerves in her ring finger were severely damaged which I believe may have been why she was hospitalized. My mother had permanent damage to her ring finger up until the day she died.

Why did he do it? I have always believed that my stepfather was jealous of the relationship my mother had with her children. He would make us stop talking to our mother and he would not allow us to speak to her in private. My stepfather did not like our mother speaking Spanish to us out of fear that we were talking about him. I believe that I completely stopped speaking my native language out of my fear of him.

I had a lot of fears as a child. My stepfather would beat my siblings and me so bad that we had welts all over our bodies. I was a skinny child, so much so that my mother was afraid to send me to school on windy days because the wind might blow me over. We never knew when the time bomb known as my stepfather would go off. He would fight my mother and wake my siblings and me up in the middle of the night to beat us for something as trivial as a dirty dish being left in the sink. One time, he threw me across the room and I hit the wall and slid down onto the floor. He would always punch my brother in his chest like he was hitting a man. My younger siblings were so terrified of him.

As the days passed, I never knew what I would come home to. There were many times he would threaten to beat me and my siblings when we got home from school. I would be in class all day afraid, thinking about the ass whooping to come while feeling ashamed, dirty and alone. I blamed myself because my stepfather would tell me it was my fault that he touched me. He would tell me that I asked for it and I could not understand why I would ask for something so horrible to happen to me.

I was nine years old when my stepfather started molesting me. I cannot tell you how traumatic that experience was for me. I did not understand what was happening to me nor why. I wondered:

- **Why does he have me laying down in their bed?**
- **Why is he touching me?**
- **Why did he take my hand to touch his thing?**
- **Why is he not stopping? Does he not hear me crying for him to please stop?**
- **What is this sensation taking over my body?**

My stepfather never penetrated me, but thoroughly enjoyed touching me and having me touch him. The sexual abuse stopped when I was 13 years old. My stepfather threatened to kill me or my mother if I ever told anyone. He repeatedly told me that my mother would not believe me and would lock me up, which convinced me to remain silent. I believed the things my stepfather told me and I kept this dirty secret for years until I reached my breaking point.

One night, when I was 16 years old, my stepfather came into my room and attempted to molest me again. I ran away from home, in shock. After all these years, how could he have the audacity to come into my room and attempt to molest me again? I wasn't nine years old anymore and the fear was gone. Something within me started to change and I started hating this man. I hated him to his core.

My stepfather didn't touch me that night because I threatened to tell my mother. I also shared his attempt with a friend of mine (who's still my friend to this day). I ran away that night because I wanted out of that family and that life, so I went to be with my boyfriend. We were living in

Panama at this time, so I am not sure where I thought I was going. All the two of us did was walk around the towns all night until my parents found me in the wee hours of the morning.

Up until this point, my mother never knew about my stepfather molesting me. (If she did, she never let me know.) However, once she found me, we had reached the point of no return.

Of course, I was lectured by my stepfather and forced to go to school. While I was in class, I was summoned to the Main Office. Once I got there, I found two Criminal Investigation Detectives (CID) waiting for me. Immediately, they took me to the hospital to be examined. After the examination, I was taken to the CID office to be questioned about my abuse and my abortion. Since my father was a service member, the CID office was located on the military base where we lived.

I was informed that my stepfather was removed from the home and placed in the barracks. I was told that he would be court-martialed and I would have to testify. When my mother returned home from visiting her parents, the CID was waiting in the parking lot for her and took her straight to their office for questioning.

That was the first time my mother heard about my stepfather molesting me. I will never forget the look on my mother's or my brother's face when they saw me for the first time after the truth was revealed. At that moment, I knew our lives were forever changed and I blamed myself.

Contrary to my belief, I was never questioned further from any legal authority. After seven days, my stepfather was released to return home. He received orders and the military moved us back to the USA. The fights between my mother and stepfather only intensified and I would jump in, attempting to protect my mother and siblings. (At this time, my mother had three more children prior to and during the start of my sexual molestation. During our fights, he would call me a liar and then say I asked for it: the molestation). I fought him anytime he was abusive to the family. I had this huge ugly monster growing inside me and I blamed him for that. My stepfather eventually left and started a new family.

My molestation for all those years resulted in my being promiscuous. I lost my virginity to two older school boys when I was 13. I didn't know what was happening at the time and I laid there numb and emotionless. Subconsciously, I expected that to happen to me. I had two abortions, one legally at age 14 and one illegally at age 15. The men I slept with ranged from age 18 to 24.

All a man had to do was tell me he loved me and I gave up the cookie. I had no self-respect; I didn't even know what it meant to respect myself. My stepfather, seeing the result of his actions on my life, lectured me about self-respect, loving myself and saving my body for the man who loved me. All I heard was *blah, blah, blah, because it was too late for that lecture. My stepfather had crossed so many boundaries and, due to his abuse, I was out there wild and loose. As bright of a student I was in school–rarely ever having to study to pass a test–was as confused as I was when it came to love and sex.*

I got pregnant again during my senior year of high school. I gave birth to my son Kevin at age 18. Kevin was my saving grace. I don't know where I would be right now if it wasn't for my son. There were several occasions when I thought of committing suicide, but as a mother, I wanted to protect my child despite my unbearable emotional pain.

My son was and is the best thing in my life. I wanted him to grow up in a home without abuse, so I married at age 19. I wanted so badly for my son to be able to speak up for himself and to know his identity. I did not want him to struggle to discover himself as I did. I did not want to inflict my hurt onto my son, so I buried and masked a lot of my pain in the guise of being a "good mother."

I believe that I had an angel for a mother and a devil for a father. I took the teachings of my mother, the strength I saw her embody, and walked with that while still masking my hurt and pain. My mother tried for years to talk to me about my abuse and I would respond, "I am good Mom." I always remained strong for my family and pushed my hurt and pain aside. My regret is I wished I had opened up to my mother before she died. This regret has been the most difficult part of my healing. I don't blame her, but I need her now more than ever in order to heal from my open wounds.

The truth is *hurt people, hurt people. I have caused some of my hurts due to* my own ordeal. Through it all, I have learned that understanding and forgiveness is the key. I forgave my stepfather for his actions before he passed away. I have forgiven myself for the choices I have made and for the nasty words I would say to myself about myself. Healing is on the horizon for me.

I have given so much of myself to others that I am in the space of learning how to give to myself. I am working on truly loving me. I am allowing healing on my terms, not based on anyone's thoughts or ideas of how my healing should look. Only by Divine Spirit am I made whole.

TELL YOUR STORY

What part of this story resonates the most with you?

_____

_____

_____

Have you seen signs of this abuse in your family?

_____

_____

_____

_____

In what ways did you respond to the trauma that was thrust upon you like this survivor?

_____

_____

_____

_____

TELL YOUR STORY (continued)

What cries went unheard (verbal and nonverbal)?

_____

_____

_____

_____

What signs of a predator were ignored?

_____

_____

_____

_____

What were your key takeaways from this survivor's story?

_____

_____

_____

_____

The Psychology Behind The Causalities of War

Gloria is a Generational Survivor of Childhood Abuse and Sexual Trauma

From an early age Gloria was placed in the role of the vicarious victim as she watched her mother being physically beaten by her step-father. She was not immune from his violent outburst and, by the age of nine, she also became a victim of molestation. The emotional abuse was further extenuated by what Gloria referred to as "psychological warfare" in that her step-father would not allow her or her siblings to communicate with their mother.

In Gloria's eyes the bond between mother and daughter was taken away and her formative years were saturated in trauma, emotional neglect and abuse. Gloria had to be the strong one by "protecting her family." Ignoring her own needs became habitual. However, over time and experience she gradually emerged as a Generational Survivor.

Dr. Sarah Williams, NCC, LPC, EAS-C

Licensed and Board Certified Clinical Psychotherapist

Clinical Trauma Specialist for *Survivors of a Generation Unheard*

Dr. Sarah's Interview with Gloria Henderson

How has the victimization affected your ability to relate to and/or trust others?

I have trust issues and sometimes I trust too much. I sometimes find it hard to express my thoughts, emotions and feelings with others. I keep a lot to myself.

Did you experience post-traumatic disorders such as Anxiety, Depression, PD, Suicidal, Self- Injury?

I have a history of suicidal thoughts, anxiety and panic related symptoms. (Side Note: These are all common due to the loss of control that occurred as a result of the abuse.)

At what point, age, stage or moment did you move from Victim to Generational Survivor?

Seeing my mom being abused and thrown through a glass door. As a survivor, I protected my family and learned to fight back. Further, I woke up and realized that the experiences of my life, although wrong, did not justify staying in a victim mentality. I no longer allow my past to determine who I am.

What steps did you take to process your healing?

Crying (is cleansing) therapy and journaling. Losing my job in 2009 was God's way of putting me on a path to becoming a Massage Therapist, which facilitated me finding my purpose and my healing. I had to forgive my Step Father. It opened me up to discovering Gloria. Being in the role of protector was removed once my Mother passed away.

What advice can you give others?

Share your story, don't keep it in. Speak your truth and do not let anyone define you. It's your truth, your walk; don't let other people tell you how to think or feel. It's okay to cry if you are hurting. You will get through it!

Clinical Perspective

Gloria has exemplified Generational Survivorship from childhood abuse and sexual trauma. For Gloria physical and sexual trauma existed, therefore she equated touch with an experience of pain.

From a clinical perspective, it would support that as a part of Gloria's healing she chose a profession that would offer healing touch (Massage Therapy). Gloria can offer healing to others which has vicarious healing to her own pain. Although Gloria's origins are ones of violent pain and abuse she has a calming spirit. She has reprocessed the pain of her past into a triumphant present.

Interview Completed by:

Dr. Sarah Williams, NCC, LPC, EAS-C
Licensed and Board Certified Clinical Psychotherapist
Clinical Trauma Specialist for *Survivors of a Generation Unheard*

Break The Stigma

I Am Not My Past
By Brandy Broward- White

Compiled by
SAADIA WHITE

SURVIVORS
— OF A —
GENERATION
UNHEARD

Stories of Generational Survivors

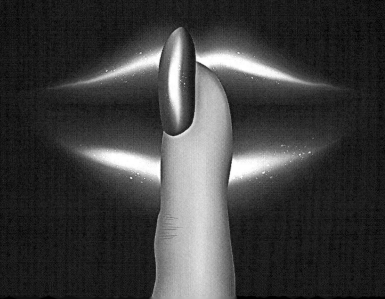

I Am Not My Past
by Brandy Broward-White

> *I am not my past. I am who I am because of my past.*

I am sharing my story to be an inspiration to all readers. Please don't feel sorry for me. What did not kill me made me stronger.

Life will take its toll on you and even beat you down to taste the dirt. I never understood why I went through what I did, let alone what my life's purpose was.

As a child all you want to do is play, watch TV and enjoy life. I experienced getting beat up as a little girl at age four. I got my first broken arm from my sister, not from playing or falling on the monkey bars. I was too young to think about my situation and what I could have done to make things better.

I couldn't understand why and, until this day, I don't know why it happened. I never knew why my sister didn't like me or what I did to make her beat me. The only reason I was given for the beatings, and anything else that my sisters did to me, was that I had a smart mouth. That was the excuse for beating me from age four to my teenage years.

When you add this to what we saw on a family trip, which I'll share with you later, I felt as if I was living without a purpose. I begin to hate and dislike them both. I remember praying to God and asking, "God, remove the hatred from my heart and help me to love the unlovable."

As I grew older, I felt an emptiness/void on the inside. Feeling so unloved, I looked for love in different relationships, only to feel worse than before. At the age of 15, I became pregnant while in the 9th grade. My child's father broke up with me during my seventh month of pregnancy. I knew nothing about how to be a mother. I was carrying my hurts, pains and unhappiness alongside my son in my womb. I had no time for a pity party, I had to figure out how to be a mother and finish high school.

Nothing was easy, but I made the best of everything. By the time I finished high school, I was pregnant again. Some might think that I should have been wiser and avoided a second pregnancy, but I was still looking for love in all the wrong places. When we look for things, we tend to find what we're looking for and it ends up being the wrong thing. We make decisions without thinking. I did a lot of that.

I finished high school with two children and raised them to the best of my ability. I married a man in my early 20s. Everything was good in the beginning until, out of nowhere, things changed. This couldn't be the same man I married, I thought.

First, we would have little fights that turned into big fights. I remember our first fight: he sat on me, strangled me and when he couldn't wrap his hands around my neck tight enough, he dragged me to the next room to wrap a belt around my neck. He was trying to kill me.

I wanted to die because I didn't think my life was going to get any better. What saved me? My son. The son I gave birth to in the ninth grade was playing outside and got into a fight with another boy. The little boy's father knocked on our apartment door while my husband was trying to kill me by tightening a belt around my neck.

The little boy's father's knocks grew louder as if he was banging on the door. My then-husband went to the door while all I could do was lay on the floor and try to catch my breath. When it was all said and done, I knew what I had to do. Of course, he said all his sorry's, that he loved me and it would never happen again.

I wore that bruise around my neck as if I was wearing a pear-shaped necklace. When I went to work, people questioned me. The bruise eventually faded after one month, but I knew I had a decision to make. For the sake of my son and daughter, I tried to end the marriage.

He would tell me things were going to get better, but they didn't. I had nothing left inside, not even one ounce of love for him. We took a trip to New York, which I thought it was like one of our regular trips to visit his family. While there he took me to a voodoo man's house. I remember thinking to myself, why are we here? Little did I know, my then-husband was determined to destroy me.

He tried to use voodoo on me which resulted in me having a nervous breakdown. I was taken to Eastern State Mental Hospital. At the time, I couldn't understand what was going on or why I was there. I was heavily medicated to the point that my vision was blurred.

I couldn't see faces nor words, only blurred colors. My mother visited me and brought my two children. I couldn't see their faces but

I remembered seeing the bright colors of my daughter's pink coat and my son's green coat. That's when I realized that I had to regain control of my life and love myself, not wasting any more time on meaningless relationships.

I was in the mental hospital for a little over three weeks. The doctor thought I was doing better and released me to go home. When my then-husband came to take me home, the doctor didn't want me to leave with him. The doctor told my mother he didn't know what was going on with me, but it had everything to do with my husband. Nevertheless, the doctor discharged me from the hospital and I went back home with my husband.

Things didn't get any better. We stayed together for about a month and when he finally left, I made sure there was no turning back. I had to gain some order in my life and be a mother to my children. Things were hard, but it was a lot better than before.

It took me a long time to understand what love really was and what it felt like. After going through everything I did with my then-husband, I realized that every man was different. They are not all the same.

I did remarry years later and never knew what it felt like to have someone love all of me. I had a wall up that had to come down so I could live my life and enjoy it to the fullest. I never used drugs nor became an alcoholic because my grandmother was an alcoholic. I saw what alcohol did to her and knew enough to know that I didn't want that. I never did drugs because my father was a drug user and I didn't want that life. Till this day if I go and hang out I only have one drink. I never finish the drink.

My experiences also affected my parenting and my relationships. I never really spanked my children, because I didn't want to hurt them, nor did I want them to feel the way I did growing up. I had unhealthy relationships because I thought fighting someone was how you showed love.

I shared my story to encourage someone that might be struggling as a generational survivor. You can overcome whatever you've been through, but you must continue to keep pushing past it. You must literally see your future as being better than your past. If it didn't kill you, it only made you stronger. You are not your past.

I love you! If you're in a relationship and you are being abused mentally, emotionally, verbally or physically, get a plan, move silently and quickly. You are a SURVIVOR as I am a Generational SURVIVOR!

TELL YOUR STORY

What part of this story resonates the most with you?

_____

_____

_____

Have you seen signs of this abuse in your family?

_____

_____

_____

In what ways did you respond to the trauma that was thrust upon you like this survivor?

_____

_____

_____

_____

TELL YOUR STORY (continued)

What cries went unheard (verbal and nonverbal)?

_____

_____

_____

_____

What signs of a predator were ignored?

_____

_____

_____

_____

What were your key takeaways from this survivor's story?

_____

_____

_____

_____

The Psychology Behind I Am Not My Past
Brandy is a Generational Survivor of Physical Abuse

It is difficult to imagine that Brandy may have survived such a horrific life experience. Brandy's life story was one of childhood physical abuse which led to adult abuse. She maintains that her life decisions were made out of her yearning for someone to love her. She experienced the agony of feelings of rejection from her father and his choice to not be close to her. However, during her interactions, she would only see him mistreating women. There were no role models to tell her how to receive or respond to love. As a result, Brandy made decisions that led her farther away from what she desired most, which was love and acceptance.

Furthermore, it was discovered late in life that the reason the person abused Brandy was because of her light skin color and sandy blond hair. Colorism in the African American community created the underpinnings of psychological harm, abuse and internal hatred. Through Brandy's journey, she was able to embrace all of the elements of her being including her skin tone.

Dr. Sarah Williams, NCC, LPC, EAS-C
Licensed and Board Certified Clinical Psychotherapist
Clinical Trauma Specialist for *Survivors of a Generation Unheard*

Dr. Sarah's Interview with Brandy Broward-White

How has the victimization affected your ability to relate to and trust others?

It took me a while. I don't trust that well. I keep people at a distance. I lash out in anger at people and have to apologize. I had to make a change and not allow myself to hurt others.

I had to pray and talk to God. I had no one to talk to about the issues. I went through life with all the hurt inside. (Per Dr. Sarah: This is a common behavior that develops from ongoing boundary violations. It's natural to want to protect the boundaries from harm.)

Did you experience post-traumatic disorders such as Anxiety, Depression, PD, Suicidal, Self- Injury?

I experienced depression from childhood to age 20. I often wished I wasn't here. I questioned why am I here if everyone is going to hurt me. I often had waves of rage. I had a battle within.

At what point, age, stage or moment did you move from Victim to Generational Survivor?

During counseling, I took a look in the mirror and realized I had to heal myself to move from the stagnancy of victimhood to survivorship.

What steps did you take to process your healing?

I read scriptures and learned methods of communication to express my hurt. I learned to talk about my feelings. In addition, I try not to ponder on the past, but live in the present.

What advice can you give others?

Find someone that will listen, leave the situation, have an exit plan. Don't mention your plans. Value your life more than anything.

Interview Completed by:
Dr. Sarah Williams, NCC, LPC, EAS-C
Licensed and Board Certified Clinical Psychotherapist
Clinical Trauma Specialist for *Survivors of a Generation Unheard*

Clinical Perspective

Brandy has exemplified Generational Survivorship from Physical Abuse. From Brandy's experience, she had to overcome the challenges associated with her father leaving and malicious abuse based upon her skin tone. How painful and confusing for Brandy to have to endure rejection and abuse throughout her life without any true explanation.

Once Brandy became a wife and a mother, she was able to resolve some of the loss and pain by giving to others what she did not receive. Brandy offers a warm and loving spirit to those around her. She healed her own rejection and pain by not only giving love, but having a willingness to accept love as well.

Dr. Sarah Williams, NCC, LPC, EAS-C
Licensed and Board Certified Clinical Psychotherapist
Clinical Trauma Specialist for *Survivors of a Generation Unheard*

Break The Stigma

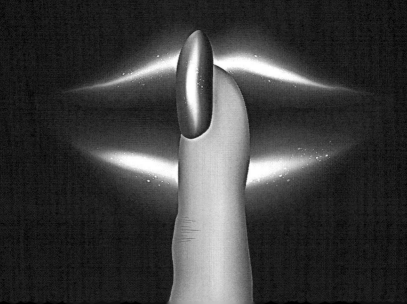

Compiled by
SAADIA WHITE

SURVIVORS
OF A
GENERATION
UNHEARD

Stories of Generational Survivors

Epilogue by Saadia White

SAADIA WHITE

I Am A
#GenerationalSurvivor

I hope you have been inspired and feel better equipped to thrive now that you have heard our tales of survival. I shared a small portion of my story, but I feel the need to share more.

To read more, please visit Amazon to purchase my e-book, I Am A #GenerationalSurvivor:

bit.ly/IAmAGenerationalSurvivorEbook

I closed my eyes and dreamed of a brighter place—a place full of colors and one where I had control. I laid there with my mother at the end of the bed, me at the front and "HIM" in the center. "HIM" was the monster, the one that told me it was okay. "HIM" asked, "You like this show?"

I was lying in front of "HIM" as a tall, lanky nine-year-old, innocent to "HIM's" monstrous ways. It felt funny, but I didn't understand what that underlying feeling was. My mother, fast asleep, had no inclination that I knew "HIM" was the monster too! She was all too familiar with "HIM's" work of dark art which I called "the hand."

He would wave his thunderous hand across my mother's light-skinned face. I called his hand a work of dark art because of all the colors it left on my mother's beautiful face—purple, black, blue and lots of red. Sometimes I would come out of my room and see his work of dark art on the bright "white walls" in the hallway. The pattern was always the same: small splatters, then large splats followed by smears made by her fingers.

I would walk down our small hall imagining I was on a school field trip, searching for smiling faces and laughter from families with small children playing about. No laughter was ever heard, just the chilling, eerie sound of "HIM's" voice along with the muffled shrills of my mother's frail whimpers.

Was this just a bad dream? No, it was a reality; my reality. I was still on the bed in front of "HIM" and my mother was fast asleep. "HIM" had positioned my hand over that hard wrinkled "thang" again. He moved my hand around the "thang". I was too stiff to move and didn't understand why he needed me to pet his "thang" for him. The television became a blur and the show was no longer my friend...

About the Compiler: Saadia White

Best-selling author and empowerment entrepreneur Saadia White, aka "The Unconventional Speaker", is no stranger to perseverance, courage and resilience. Her mission has always been to serve. From former law enforcement officer to today's modern activist, she brings her words of encouragement and wisdom to the masses as the *Amazine Amazon*.

Out of pain, she birthed her PASSION!

Saadia White is a wife, mother, grandmother and all the above, but most of all a Generational Survivor. She is an inspirational speaker and community activist with a mission of service. Through her animated SHERO, Amazine Amazon, White reaches new heights as a fearless heroin who shines a light on confidence and unconditional love as a way to turn on our lights of PURPOSE. Today, you can find her hosting free community empowerment events and continuing her campaign of perseverance through her Amazine Amazon animated collection.

For more information, please visit:

- https://www.amazineamazon.com/
- FB: @generationalsurvivors
  @amazineamazon @EWOEPG
- IG: amazineamazon gensurvivors
- Twitter: @GenSurvivors
  @AmazineAmazon
- For Speaking, Talent, Clinical Consultation, please email:
  generationalsurvivor1@gmail.com

About our book's Clinical Trauma Specialist: Dr. Sarah Williams

The therapist to celebrities, executives and professional athletes, Dr. Sarah Williams is a Licensed and Board Certified Clinical Psychotherapist, owner of Covenant Way Clinical Counseling, Polished Public Speaker and TV/Media Host. Dr. Williams' mission is to help individuals cope with mental health as well as offer a platform for individuals to share their stories of overcoming and triumph with the primary goal of letting the world know that they are not alone.

As the Host and Creator of the Mental Health TV show "Dr. Sarah After Dark", she offers a platform for guests to share their stories of overcoming life challenges. Celebrity guests can offer inspiration to others as well as lift the stigma of mental illness, bringing others from darkness to light.

Individuals in positions of leadership or celebrity status are often presented with multiple roles and responsibilities that can result in unique stressors on their lives and relationships. Seeking therapy can also be challenging due to limitations such as time or confidentiality concerns. To meet these unique challenges, Dr. Williams is trained and experienced to offer clinical services that are sensitive to the celebrity and elite client. Her services include individual, marriage/family, substance abuse counseling, group therapy and counseling to the professional athlete.

For more information, please visit:

- http://covenantwayclinicalcounseling.com
  IAmDrSarahWilliams.com
- FB: @iamdrsarahwilliams
  IG: Drsarah.w
- Twitter: @DrSarahWT1
- YouTube: bit.ly/DrSarahWilliamsYoutube
- Dr. Sarah After Dark TV Show
- For Speaking, Talent, Clinical Consultation, please email:
  iamdrsarahtv@gmail.com

Compiled by
SAADIA WHITE

SURVIVORS
— OF A —
GENERATION
UNHEARD

Stories of Generational Survivors

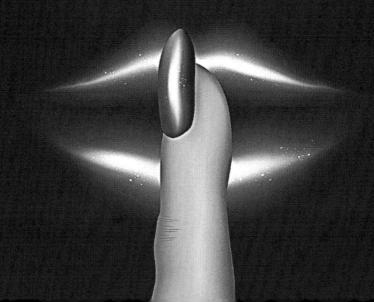

RESOURCES

The following are a list of resources for help:

General Information

- **Covenant Way Clinical Counseling:**
  http://covenantwayclinicalcounseling.com 757-606-0971
- **National Sexual Assault Hotline**: 1-800-656-HOPE
  https://www.rainn.org/about-national-sexual-assault-
  telephone-hotline
- **National Organization for Victim Assistance:**
  1-800-TRY-NOVA (879-6682)
  https://www.trynova.org/who-we-are/
- **National Online Resource Center on Violence Against
  Women:** 1-800-537-2238 https://vawnet.org/
- **U.S. Department of Justice: National Sex Offender Public
  Website:** https://www.nsopw.gov/
- **The National Center for Victims of Crime:**
  https://victimsofcrime.org/
- **National Street Harassment Hotline:**
  1-855-897-5910
  http://www.stopstreetharassment.org/our-work/
  nationalshhotline/

RESOURCES (continued)

Child Abuse/Sexual Abuse

- **National Child Abuse Hotline:** 1-800-4-A-CHILD (422-4453)
  https://www.childhelp.org/
- **Darkness to Light:** 1-866-FOR-LIGHT (367-5444)
  https://www.d2l.org/
- **National Center for Missing and Exploited Children:**
  1-800-THE-LOST (843-5678)
  https://report.cybertip.org/index.htm
- **National Children's Alliance:**
  https://www.nationalchildrensalliance.org/
- **Stop It Now:** 1-888-PREVENT (773-8368)
  https://www.stopitnow.org/
- **Justice for Children:** https://justiceforchildren.org/

Domestic, Dating And Intimate Partner Violence

- **National Domestic Violence Hotline:** 1-800-799-SAFE
  https://www.thehotline.org/
- **National Teen Dating Abuse Online Helpline:**
  1-866-331-9474   https://www.loveisrespect.org/
- **Pathways to Safety International:**
  https://pathwaystosafety.org/
- **National Coalition against Domestic Violence:**
  http://www.ncadv.org/

RESOURCES (continued)

Incest

- **Survivors of Incest Anonymous:** https://siawso.org/
- **GirlThrive:** https://www.invisiblegirlsthrive.com/

Stalking

- **Stalking Resource Center:** https://victimsofcrime.org/our-programs/past-programs/stalking-resource-center

Survivors With Disabilities

- **Deaf Abused Women's Network (DAWN):** 1-202-559-5366 http://deafdawn.org/
- **CAVANET:** http://cavnet.blogspot.com/
- **National disability rights network:** https://www.ndrn.org/

College Students

- **NotAlone.gov**
- **Know Your IX:** https://www.knowyourix.org/
- **End Rape on Campus:** https://endrapeoncampus.org/

Resources For Male Survivors Of Sexual Assault

- **1in6:** https://1in6.org/
- **Jimhopper.com**
- **Malesurvivor.org**

RESOURCES (continued)

LGBTQ Survivors

- **GLBTQ Domestic Violence Project:** 1-800-832-1901
  http://www.glbtqdvp.org/
- **the Network la Red:** 1-617-742-4911   http://tnlr.org/en/
- **National Coalition of Anti-Violence Programs:**
  1-212-714-1141   https://avp.org/
- **The Trevor Project:** 1-866-488-7386
  https://www.thetrevorproject.org/
- **GLBT National Hotline:** 1-888-THE-GLNH (843-4564)
  http://www.glbtnationalhelpcenter.org/
- **FORGE (For Ourselves: Reworking Gender Expression):**
  https://forge-forward.org/
- **Association for Lesbian, Gay, Bisexual & Transgender Issues in Counseling:** http://algbtic.org/therapist-resource-listing.html

Human Trafficking

- **National Human Trafficking Resource Center:**
  1-888-373-7888
- **U.S. Department of Justice Trafficking in Persons and Worker Exploitation Complaint Line:** 1-888-428-7581

Military Resources:

- **Safe Helpline:** 1-877-995-5247

RESOURCES (continued)

Legal Resources:

- **Womenslaw.org**
- **The Laws in Your State:** https://apps.rainn.org/policy/
- **Attorney Referral Line:** 1-202-467-8716
  https://victimsofcrime.org/our-programs/national-crime-victim-bar-association/for-victims
- **Take Back The Night Foundation:** 1-866-966-9013
  https://takebackthenight.org/
- **It Happened to Alexa Foundation:**
  https://www.ithappenedtoalexa.org/
- **U.S. Department of Justice, Civil Rights Division:**
  1-844-380-6178 or fairhousing@usdoj.gov.
  https://www.justice.gov/crt/housing-and-civil-enforcement-section

Medical/Physical Health:

- **Sexual Assault Nurse Examiner (SANE):** 1-877-464-4772
  https://www.sane-sart.com/
- **Healthcare Center Directory:** 1-877-464-4772
  https://findahealthcenter.hrsa.gov/
- **The Center For Disease Control National Prevention Information Network (AIDS/HIV, STI Information):**
  1-800-458-5231   https://npin.cdc.gov/
- **International Association of Forensic Nurses:**
  https://www.forensicnurses.org/default.aspx
- **Start Your Recovery:**
  https://startyourrecovery.org/experiences/sexual-assault

RESOURCES (continued)

Mental Health:

- **Sidran Traumatic Stress Foundation:**
  https://www.sidran.org/
- **GoodTherapy.org:** GoodTherapy.org
- **Psychology Today:**
  https://www.psychologytoday.com/us/treatment-rehab
- **National Eating Disorder Helpline:** 1-800-931-2237
  https://www.nationaleatingdisorders.org/
- **National Alliance on Mental Illness (NAMI):**
  1-888-950-NAMI (6264)   https://www.nami.org/
- **Hope Exists After Rape Trauma:**
  https://h-e-a-r-t.org/about-us/

Sexual Assault Prevention:

- **National Violence Against Women Prevention Research Center:** https://mainweb-v.musc.edu/vawprevention/
- **Project Respect:** https://www.yesmeansyes.com/
- **PreventConnect:** http://www.preventconnect.org/
- **Campus Outreach Services:**
  https://campusoutreachservices.com/
- **The Date Safe Project:** https://www.centerforrespect.com/
- **Child Help: Speak Up Be Safe:** https://www.childhelp.org/subs/childhelp-speak-up-be-safe/
- **Men Can Stop Rape:** https://mcsr.org/
- **Cyber Bullying Research Center:**
  https://cyberbullying.org/

RESOURCES (continued)

International Sexual Assault Resources

◆ **For Americans Living Abroad**

     o   Get help in an emergency by locating the nearest Embassy or Consulate. You can also call the State Department's emergency numbers:

         »   From the U.S. & Canada 1-888-407-4747

         »   From Overseas +1-202-501-4444

JOIN The Movement!

www.facebook.com/generationalsurvivors

TheGenerationalSurvivors.com

https://www.facebook.com/EWOEPG/

Made in the USA
Columbia, SC
10 June 2020

98754511R10046